D1716254

A New True Book

NEWSPAPERS

By David Petersen

This "true book" was prepared
under the direction of
Illa Podendorf,
formerly with the Laboratory School,
University of Chicago

 CHILDRENS PRESS, CHICAGO

Library of Congress Cataloging in Publication Data

Petersen, David.
  Newspapers.

  (A New true book)
  Includes index.
  Summary: Describes the history and purpose of newspapers, the organization of a newspaper office, the various people who put a newspaper together, and how newspapers are distributed. Also includes a glossary of terms.
  1. Newspapers—Juvenile literature. [1. Newspapers]
I. Title. II. Series.
PN4776.P47 1983   070   83-10069
ISBN 0-516-01702-0   AACR2

TABLE OF CONTENTS

What Is a Newspaper?...5

Types of Newspapers...7

The History of Newspapers...10

Penny Newspapers...18

How Does a Newspaper Work?...21

News Services...32

Newspapers Around the World...37

Newspaper Careers...45

Words You Should Know...46

Index...47

WHAT IS A NEWSPAPER?

A newspaper is just what its name says—news printed on paper. More people find out what is going on in the world from newspapers than from any other source, even television.

More people read newspapers every day in Sweden than in any other country in the world. Japan, East Germany, and Finland also have a high number of people who read a paper every day.

In America, more than nine out of every ten adults read a newspaper every day. Newspapers also educate, entertain, and perform public services for their readers.

TYPES OF NEWSPAPERS

There are many different types of newspapers.

A newspaper that is published at least once every day is called a daily.

There are two kinds of daily newspapers: morning and evening. Each of these is called an edition. Most daily newspapers publish a special Sunday edition.

Collection of publications that are printed
daily, weekly, or monthly

Some newspapers
publish only one edition
each week. These are
called weeklies, or weekly
newspapers.

There are also special-interest newspapers. A special-interest newspaper usually deals with only one particular subject. There are special newspapers for businesses, schools, churches, clubs, and hobbies. The *Wall Street Journal* is a special-interest paper. Every day more than two million people read this paper.

THE HISTORY OF NEWSPAPERS

People who gather news and write stories for newspapers are called reporters. The first reporters were people who traveled about telling the news in songs or poems. These songs and poems were called ballads.

Gutenberg, the German who invented the method of printing from moveable type, looks at the first page of the Bible he printed.

Then the printing press was invented. A printing press is a machine that prints many copies of something.

Printer checking newspaper on press

Think how long it would take one person to write out all the news in just one copy of one newspaper! A printing press does that big job in only a few seconds.

The first real newspaper was printed in London, England, in 1665. It was called the *London Gazette.* The word *gazette* used to mean "official publication." Today, many newspapers use gazette as part of their name.

The word *newspaper* also comes from England. It was first used in 1670.

The first daily newspaper was published in London in 1702. It was called the *Daily Courant.*

America had its first printing press in the 1630s. But the first successful American newspaper wasn't printed until 1704. It was called the *Boston News-Letter.*

N. E.　　　　　　　　　Numb. 17

The Boston News-Letter.

Publiſhed by Authority.

From **Monday** April 17. to **Monday** April 24. 1704.

London Flying-Poſt from Decemb. 2d. to 4th. 1703

Letters from *Scotland* bring us the Copy of a Sheet lately Printed there, Intituled, *A ſeaſonable Alarm for* Scotland. *In a Letter from a Gentleman in the City, to his Friend in the Country, concerning the preſent Danger of the Kingdom and of the Proteſtant Religion.*

This Letter takes Notice. That Papiſts ſwarm in that Nation, that they traffick more avowedly than formerly, and that of Late many Scores of Prieſts & Jeſuites are come thither from France, and gone to the North, to the Highlands & other places of the Country. That the Miniſters of the Highlands and North gave in large Liſts of them to the Committee of the General Aſſembly, to be laid before the Privy-Council

It likewiſe obſerves, that a great Number of other ill-affected perſons are come over from France, under pretence of accepting her Majeſty's Gracious Indemnity, but, in, reality, to increaſe Diviſions in The Nation, and to entertain a Correſpondence with France: That their ill Intentions are evident from their talking big, their owning the Intereſt of the pretended King James VIII. their ſecret Cabals, and their buying up of Arms and Ammunition, wherever they can find them.

To this he adds the late Writings and Actings of ſome diſaffected perſons, many of whom are for that Pretender, that ſeveral of them have declar'd they had rather embrace Popery than conform to the preſent Government, that they refuſe to pray for the Queen, but uſe the ambiguous word Soveraign, and ſome of them pray in expreſs Words for the King and Royal Family, and the charming and generous Prince who has ſhew'd them Kindneſs. He likewiſe takes notice of ſomething ago found in Cypher, & ...

From all this he infers, That they have hopes of Aſſiſtance from *France*, otherwiſe they would never be ſo impudent, and he gives Reaſons for his Apprehenſions that the French King may ſend Troops thither this Winter, 1 Becauſe the Engliſh & Dutch will not then be at Sea to oppoſe them. 2. He can then beſt ſpare them, the Seaſon of Action beyond Sea being over. 3 The Expectation given him of a conſiderable number to joyn them, may incourage him to the undertaking with fewer Men, if he can but ſend over a ſufficient number of Officers with Arms and Ammunition.

He endeavours in the reſt of his Letters to anſwer the fooliſh Pretences of the Pretender's being a Proteſtant, and that he will govern us according to Law. He ſays, that being bred up in the Religion and Politicks of France, he is by Education a ſtated Enemy to our Liberty and Religion. That the Obligations which he and his Family owe to the French King muſt neceſſarily make him to be wholly at his Devotion, and to follow his Example; that if he be upon the Throne, the three Nations muſt be oblig'd to pay the Debt which he owes the French King for the Education of himſelf, and ſor Entertaining his ſuppoſed Father and his Family. And ſince the King muſt reſtore him by his Troops, if ever he be reſtored, he will ſee to ſecure his own Debt, before thoſe Troops leave Britain. The Pretender being a good Proficient in the French and Romiſh Schools, he will never think himſelf ſufficiently aveng'd, but by the utter Ruine of his Proteſtant Subjects, both as Hereticks and Traitors. The late Queen, his pretended Mother, who in cold Blood when ſhe was Queen of Britain, adviſ'd to turn the Weſt of Scotland into a hunting Field, will be then for doing ſo by the greateſt part of the Nation, and, no doubt, is at Pains to have her preſent educated to her own Mind Therefore ... a great M ...

This newspaper was very small. It was about the size of one sheet of notebook paper, with printing on both sides.

One person did all the jobs on early newspapers. This person was the reporter, the editor, the printer, and the seller.

Benjamin Franklin at a printing press

Benjamin Franklin ran a one-man newspaper.

Most of the news in the first American newspapers was taken from the larger English newspapers. They were brought to America on sailing ships. The ships traveled very slowly. By the time the English news was printed and read in American newspapers, it was several months old!

PENNY NEWSPAPERS

In 1833, the *New York Sun* became the first penny newspaper. Penny newspapers were very much like today's newspapers. They printed the news while it was still new. They were the first newspapers to print advertisements.

Penny newspapers were also the first to use street

sales. Street sales include
newsstands and newspaper
machines. Penny newspapers
were the first to use carriers.
They deliver newspapers
to people's houses.

Many newspaper stands sell magazines and candy, too.

Today there are almost ten thousand different newspapers in the United States. About 61 million copies of these newspapers are printed every day!

HOW DOES A NEWSPAPER WORK?

Every newspaper has three departments, or parts. They are: editorial, mechanical, and business.

The editorial department's most important job is to gather the news. A person who gathers the news is called a reporter. A reporter also writes stories about the news he or she has gathered.

Photographer takes pictures of a parade
for his newspaper.

A photographer takes
pictures to go with the
reporter's stories.
Sometimes, the reporter
and the photographer are
the same person.

Left: At the Chicago Tribune
reporters and editors use video
display terminals to write
and edit stories. Later their
stories will be set in
type by computers.
Above: An editor discusses
a story with a reporter.

The editor reads the
reporters' stories to make
sure they are correct. The
editor looks for mistakes in
spelling and makes sure
the facts in the stories are
right.

The editor also decides how important a story is. An important story might appear on the front page. Stories that are not as important would probably be on the inside pages.

Sometimes the editor decides a story should not appear in the paper at all.

The second department of a newspaper is the mechanical department. This department sees that the news gets printed.

The typesetter works on a linotype machine.
When he types out the story raised metal letters
drop into position filling a line of type at a time.

The reporters' stories are put in type. This is called typesetting. The photographers' pictures are developed. Then the type and the pictures are put in place. They follow the layout made by the editorial department.

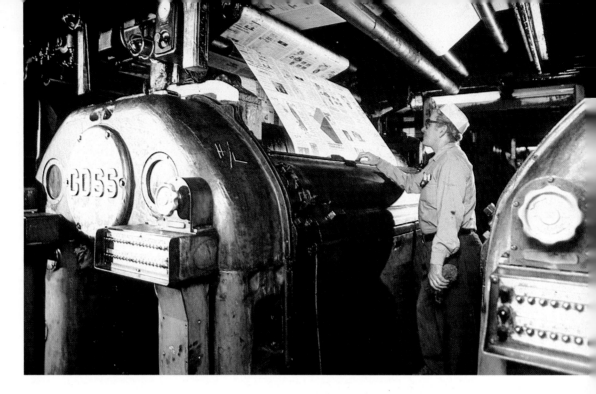

A printer has stopped the press to check a press sheet. Newspaper presses are big. The metroliner press (below) can print 75,000 papers in an hour. It can print using all four colors—red, yellow, blue, black—or only one color, black. This book has been printed on a smaller four-color press.

The biggest job of the mechanical department is the printing of the newspaper. Some small newspapers send their work to outside printing shops. But most large newspapers have their own printing presses.

After an issue, or edition, of a newspaper has been printed, it is ready to be sold, or circulated.

The third department of a newspaper is the business department. It takes care of all the business of the newspaper.

One job of the business department is to sell advertising space. Advertising is very important for newspapers.

Collection of newspaper ads.

Many newspapers make
more money from selling
advertising space than they
do from selling newspapers.

Trucks deliver papers to all parts of the city. But in many places, papers are delivered to homes by carriers on bikes.

Another job of the business department is to sell the newspapers. Some newspapers are sold in stores and from newsstands. Others are sold from machines. But most newspapers are

delivered directly to
people's homes by carriers.

Some newspapers are
delivered through the mail.
That's because people
often like to read
newspapers that are
printed in other parts of
the state, country, or world.

The business department
also takes care of normal
business jobs, such as
paying the bills and
keeping records.

NEWS SERVICES

Modern newspapers can print news from anywhere in the world, almost as soon as it happens. This speedy news is made possible by a machine called a teletype.

The word *teletype* is a combination of the words *telegraph* and *typewriter.*

Operators sort teletype messages received from wire services.

When a news event takes place somewhere, the story is typed into a machine. This machine sends the story to newspapers throughout the world.

33

The organizations that
send news stories over
teletype machines are
called news services.
Because the teletype
sends messages through
wires, the news services
are sometimes called wire
services.

In the United States,
there are two main news
services. One is called the
Associated Press. Stories
sent to a newspaper by
the Associated Press have

An editor calls up a reporter's story on his terminal for a final edit.

the letters AP at the beginning of the story.

The other big news service is called United Press International. Its initials are UPI.

All large American newspapers are members of either the AP or UPI news service. Some newspapers belong to both.

Newspaper stand in Casablanca

NEWSPAPERS AROUND THE WORLD

There is some sort of newspaper in almost every country in the world.

Canada has more than one hundred daily newspapers and over eight hundred weekly papers.

Japan has almost two hundred daily newspapers. The biggest newspapers in Japan are *Asahi*

Shimbun, *Mainichi Shimbun*, and *Yomiuri Shimbun*.

The People's Republic of China has the largest population of any country in the world. But China has fewer than four hundred daily newspapers.

The largest of the Chinese newspapers is called *Jen Min Jih Pao* (People's Daily). It is published in China's capital city, Beijing.

Typesetter sets type for a publisher in New Delhi, the capital of India.

China sometimes claims to have had the first printed newspaper in the world. It was started in the year 618, and was called *Ti-pao*. *Ti* means "palace" and *pao* means "report."

This early Chinese palace report was used to send messages between officials. A real newspaper is used to spread news to all the people. So the *Ti-pao* can't really be called a newspaper. It might be more accurate to say that the *Ti-pao* was the earliest ancestor of modern newspapers.

Newspapers are very popular in most European

While he waits for customers, a worker reads a newspaper in Liberty Market in Guadalajara, Mexico.

countries. France, for example, has well over a hundred daily newspapers.

Paris, the capital city of France, has about a dozen daily newspapers of its own.

Even most of the smallest countries in Africa have newspapers.

The two largest newspapers in the world are printed in London, England.

The *London Daily Mirror* and the *London Daily Express* each print about four million copies every day!

The largest newspaper in the United States is the New York *Daily News.*

The *News* has sales, usually called circulation,

Big cities often have three or four different newspapers published every day.

of over 2 million copies each day.

Newspapers are popular everywhere. People like to know what is happening nearby and in other parts of the world.

NEWSPAPER CAREERS

Working for a newspaper can be exciting. There are many different kinds of jobs.

Perhaps you might someday be a reporter, a photographer, an editor, an advertising seller, or a printer!

The next time you read a newspaper, think about all the different people who worked together to make it.

WORDS YOU SHOULD KNOW

These are special words used by people in the newspaper business.

assignment(ah • SINE • ment)—an event or subject that is "assigned" to a particular reporter for coverage

beat(BEET)—an area of interest assigned to a reporter for regular coverage. Some beats are: sports, politics, schools, and religion.

bulletin(BULL • ih • tin)—an important news item, usually inserted in an issue of a newspaper just before it goes to press; a "last-minute bulletin"

by-line(BY • lyne)—the reporter's name placed above a story

caption(KAP • shun)—a written explanation placed below a photograph or other illustration, sometimes called a "cut-line"

column(KAHL • um)—a regular feature in a newspaper, usually written by the same person each time

copy(KAH • pea)—any written material in a newspaper; copy includes stories, advertisements, and photo captions

correspondent(KOR • is • PON • dint)—a reporter whose "beat" is located in a different town, state, or country than the one in which his newspaper is based. "New York correspondent," "Our man in Europe," etc.

deadline(DED • lyne)—the date or hour by which a particular issue of a newspaper must go to the printer, or by which a reporter must submit his or her stories to the editor for approval

edition(eh • DISH • un)—a particular issue of a newspaper; standard editions are morning, evening, and Sunday. When a particularly newsworthy event takes place, some newspapers publish special editions, called "extras."

five ws(FYVE • DUB • il • y ɔoz)—"Who, What, When, Where, Why?" The facts that a good news story will always contain.

freelance(FREE • lanss)—a writer or photographer who does not work for a particular newspaper, but rather, sells stories or photos to several different publications

headline(HED • lyne) — the title of a newspaper story, usually appearing in large type at the top of the story

italics(eye • TAL • ix) — a *slanted* typeface, used to give certain words special meaning or emphasis

justified type(JUSS • tih • fyed • TIPE) — columns of type that are even on both left and right sides. Newspapers use justified type for neatness.

libel(LYE • bil) — a false statement appearing in print

masthead(MAST • hed) — a boxed-in section appearing in each edition of a newspaper. The masthead gives vital information about the newspaper — such as the names of the publisher and editor, the address of the newspaper's business offices, etc.

press(PRESS) — a term applied to all newspapers collectively, as in "The press gave favorable reviews of the new book."

proofreader(PROOF • reader) — a person who checks written copy for errors, usually the proofreader is an editor.

publisher(PUB • lish • er) — the person in charge of the business functions of a newspaper. Often the publisher is also the owner.

scoop(SKOOP) — an important story reported in one newspaper before other newspapers know about it

INDEX

adult readership, 6
advertisements, 18, 28, 29
Africa, 42
Asahi Shimbun, 37, 38
Associated Press (AP), 34, 35
ballads, 10
Beijing, China, 38
Boston News-Letter, 14, 15
business department, 21, 28-31
Canada, 37
careers, 45
carriers, 19, 31
China, 38-40

circulation, 27, 42
Daily Courant, 14
daily newspapers, 7, 14
editions, 7, 8, 27
editorial department, 21-24, 25
editors, 16, 23, 24
England, 13, 14, 17, 42
evening newspapers, 7
first American newspaper, 14
first daily newspaper, 14
first newspaper, 13
first penny newspaper, 18
foreign newspapers, 13, 14, 37-43

France, 41
Franklin, Benjamin, 17
gazette, definition, 13
history of newspapers, 10-17
issues, 27
Japan, 37
Jen Min Jih Pao, 38
layout, 25
London, England, 13, 14, 42
London Daily Express, 42
London Daily Mirror, 42
London Gazette, 13
mail delivery, 31
Mainichi Shimbun, 38
mechanical department, 21, 24-27
morning newspapers, 7
newspaper, definition, 5-6
newspaper, first use of word, 13
newspaper machines, 19, 30
news services, 32-35
newsstands, 19, 30
New York Daily News, 42
New York Sun, 18
one-man newspapers, 16, 17
palace report, Chinese, 39, 40

Paris, France, 41
penny newspapers, 18, 19
People's Republic of China, 38
photographers, 22, 25
printers, 16
printing presses, 11, 12, 14, 27
reporters, 10, 16, 21-23, 25
sellers, 16
selling, 27, 30
special-interest newspapers, 9
street sales, 18-19
Sunday newspaper, 7
telegraph, 32
teletype machines, 32-34
television, 5
Ti-pao, 39, 40
typesetting, 25
United Press International (UPI), 35
United States of America, 6, 14, 17, 20, 34, 35, 42
Wall Street Journal, 9
weekly newspapers (weeklies), 8
wire services, 34
Yomiuri Shimbun, 38

About the Author

David Petersen is a freelance writer living in Durango, Colorado. Before going freelance, David spent several years as managing editor of a small magazine based in California. He has had over 100 articles published in a variety of magazines and newspapers throughout the country.

In addition to his professional writing and editing, David teaches writing at Fort Lewis College in Durango. He holds a B.A. in Social Sciences from Chapman College in Orange, California; and a B.A. in Creative Writing from Fort Lewis.